AF433375

Seashells
One Year
Organizational
Planner

20__

Year at a Glance

January – June

Month	Sunday	Monday	Tuesday	Wednesday	Thursday	Friday	Saturday
January							
February							
March							
April							
May							
June							

July – December

Month	Sunday	Monday	Tuesday	Wednesday	Thursday	Friday	Saturday
July							
August							
September							
November							
December							

20__
Year at a Glance

January - June

Month	Sunday	Monday	Tuesday	Wednesday	Thursday	Friday	Saturday
January							
February							
March							
April							
May							
June							

July – December

Month	Sunday	Monday	Tuesday	Wednesday	Thursday	Friday	Saturday
July							
August							
September							
November							
December							

20__

Year at a Glance

January - June

Month	Sunday	Monday	Tuesday	Wednesday	Thursday	Friday	Saturday
January							
February							
March							
April							
May							
June							

July – December

Month	Sunday	Monday	Tuesday	Wednesday	Thursday	Friday	Saturday
July							
August							
September							
November							
December							

August 20__ At a Glance

	Sunday	Monday	Tuesday	Wednesday	Thursday	Friday	Saturday
	Sunday	Monday	Tuesday	Wednesday	Thursday	Friday	Saturday

September 20 __ At A Glance

	Sunday	Monday	Tuesday	Wednesday	Thursday	Friday	Saturday

October 20__ At A Glance

	Sunday	Monday	Tuesday	Wednesday	Thursday	Friday	Saturday

November 20__ At A Glance

	Sunday	Monday	Tuesday	Wednesday	Thursday	Friday	Saturday

December 20__ At A Glance

	Sunday	Monday	Tuesday	Wednesday	Thursday	Friday	Saturday

August 20 __ Monthly Planner

Key Points	Sunday	Monday	Tuesday	Wednesday	Thursday	Friday	Saturday
Key Points							
Remember to Do							

August __ - __, 20__ Weekly Planner

	Sunday	Monda	Tuesda	Wednes	Thursd	Friday	Saturd
Period							
Class							
Time							
Period							
Class							
Time							
Period							
Class							
Time							

August __ - __, 20__ Weekly Planner

	Sunday	Monda	Tuesda	Wednes	Thursd	Friday	Saturd
Period Class Time							
Period Class Time							
	Sunday	Monda	Tuesda	Wednes	Thursd	Friday	Saturd

August __ - __, 20__ Weekly Planner

	Sunday	Monda	Tuesda	Wednes	Thursd	Friday	Saturd
Period Class Time							
	Sunday	Monda	Tuesda	Wednes	Thursd	Friday	Saturd

August __-__, 20__ Weekly Planner

	Sunday	Monda	Tuesda	Wednes	Thursd	Friday	Saturd
Period Class Time							

August __ - __, 20__ Weekly Planner

	Sunday	Monda	Tuesda	Wednes	Thursd	Friday	Saturd
Period Class Time							

September 20__ Monthly Planner

Key Points	Sunday	Monday	Tuesday	Wednesday	Thursday	Friday	Saturday
Remember To Do							

September __ - __, 20__ Weekly Planner

	Sunda	Monda	Tuesda	Wednes	Thurs	Friday	Saturd
Period Class Time							
Period Class Time							
	Sunda	Monda	Tuesda	Wednes	Thurs	Friday	Saturd

September __-__, 20__ Weekly Planner

		Sunda	Monda	Tuesda	Wednes	Thurs	Friday	Saturd
Period Class Time								
Period Class Time								
		Sunda	Monda	Tuesda	Wednes	Thurs	Friday	Saturd

September __-__, 20__ Weekly Planner

	Sunda	Monda	Tuesda	Wednes	Thurs	Friday	Saturd
Period Class Time							
Period Class Time							
Period Class Time	Sunda	Monda	Tuesda	Wednes	Thurs	Friday	Saturd

September __ - __, 20__ Weekly Planner

	Sunda	Monda	Tuesda	Wednes	Thurs	Friday	Saturd
Period Class Time							
Period Class Time	Sunda	Monda	Tuesda	Wednes	Thurs	Friday	Saturd

September __ - __, 20 __ Weekly Planner

	Sunda	Monda	Tuesda	Wednes	Thurs	Friday	Saturd
Period Class Time							
Period Class Time	Sunda	Monda	Tuesda	Wednes	Thurs		Saturd

October 20__ Monthly Planner

Key Points	Sunday	Monday	Tuesday	Wednesday	Thursday	Friday	Saturday
Remember to Do							

October __ - __, 20__ Weekly Planner

	Sunday	Monday	Tuesday	Wednesday	Thursday	Friday	Saturday
Period Class Time							

	Sunday	Monday	Tuesday	Wednesday	Thursday	Friday	Saturday
Period Class Time							

October __ - __, 20__ Weekly Planner

	Sunday	Monday	Tuesday	Wednesday	Thursday	Friday	Saturday
Period Class Time							
Period Class Time							

October __ - __, 20__ Weekly Planner

	Sunday	Monday	Tuesday	Wednesday	Thursday	Friday	Saturday
Period Class Time							

October __ - __, 20__ Weekly Planner

	Sunday	Monday	Tuesday	Wednesday	Thursday	Friday	Saturday
Period Class Time							

October __ - __, 20 __ Weekly Planner

	Sunday	Monday	Tuesday	Wednesday	Thursday	Friday	Saturday
Period Class Time							

November 20__ Monthly Planner

	Sunday	Monday	Tuesday	Wednesday	Thursday	Friday	Saturday
Key Points							
Remember To Do							

November __ - __, 20__ Weekly Planner

	Sunday	Monday	Tuesday	Wednesday	Thursday	Friday	Saturday
Period Class Time							

	Sunday	Monday	Tuesday	Wednesday	Thursday	Friday	Saturday
Period Class Time							

November __ - __, 20__ Weekly Planner

	Sunday	Monday	Tuesday	Wednesday	Thursday	Friday	Saturday
Period Class Time							
Period Class Time							

November __ - __, 20 __ Weekly Planner

	Sunday	Monday	Tuesday	Wednesday	Thursday	Friday	Saturday
Period Class Time							
	Sunday	Monday	Tuesday	Wednesday	Thursday	Friday	Saturday
Period Class Time							

November __ - __, 20__ Weekly Planner

	Sunday	Monday	Tuesday	Wednesday	Thursday	Friday	Saturday
Period Class Time							
	Sunday	Monday	Tuesday	Wednesday	Thursday	Friday	Saturday
Period Class Time							

November __ - __, 20 __ Weekly Planner

	Sunday	Monday	Tuesday	Wednesday	Thursday	Friday	Saturday
Period Class Time							
	Sunday	Monday	Tuesday	Wednesday	Thursday	Friday	Saturday
Period Class Time							

December 20__ Monthly Planner

	Sunday	Monday	Tuesday	Wednesday	Thursday	Friday	Saturday
Key Points							
Remember To Do							

December __ - __, 20__ Weekly Planner

		Sunday	Monday	Tuesday	Wednesday	Thursday	Saturday
Period Class Time							
		Sunday	Monday	Tuesday	Wednesday	Thursday	Saturday
Period Class Time							

December __ ~ __, 20__ Weekly Planner

	Sunday	Monday	Tuesday	Wednesday	Thursday	Friday	Saturday
Period Class Time							
	Sunday	Monday	Tuesday	Wednesday	Thursday	Friday	Saturday
Period Class Time							

December __ - __, 20__ Weekly Planner

	Sunday	Monday	Tuesday	Wednesday	Thursday	Friday	Saturday
Period Class Time							
	Sunday	Monday	Tuesday	Wednesday	Thursday	Friday	Saturday
Period Class Time							

December __ - __, 20__ Weekly Planner

	Sunday	Monday	Tuesday	Wednesday	Thursday	Friday	Saturday
Period Class Time							
	Sunday	Monday	Tuesday	Wednesday	Thursday	Friday	Saturday
Period Class Time							

December __ - __, 20__ Weekly Planner

	Sunday	Monday	Tuesday	Wednesday	Thursday	Friday	Saturday
Period Class Time							
		Sunday	Monday	Tuesday	Wednesday	Thursday	Friday	Saturday
Period Class Time							

December __ - __, 20__ Weekly Planner

		Sunday	Monday	Tuesday	Wednesday	Thursday	Friday	Saturday
Period Class Time								
		Sunday	Monday	Tuesday	Wednesday	Thursday	Friday	Saturday
Period Class								

20__
Year at a
Glance

January ~ June

Month	Sunday	Monday	Tuesday	Wednesday	Thursday	Friday	Saturday
January							
February							
March							
April							
May							
June							

July – December

Month	Sunday	Monday	Tuesday	Wednesday	Thursday	Friday	Saturday
July							
August							
September							
November							
December							

January 20__ Monthly Planner

Key Points	Sunday	Monday	Tuesday	Wednesday	Thursday	Friday	Saturday
Remember To Do							

February 20__ Monthly Planner

Key Points	Sunday	Monday	Tuesday	Wednesday	Thursday	Friday	Saturday
Remember To Do							

March 20__ Monthly Planner

Key Points	Sunday	Monday	Tuesday	Wednesday	Thursday	Friday	Saturday
Key Points							
Remember To Do							

April 20__ Monthly Planner

Key Points	Sunday	Monday	Tuesday	Wednesday	Thursday	Friday	Saturday
Remember To Do							

May 20__ Monthly Planner

Key Points	Sunday	Monday	Tuesday	Wednesday	Thursday	Friday	Saturday
Key Points	Sunday	Monday	Tuesday	Wednesday	Thursday	Friday	Saturday
Remember To Do							

June 20__ Monthly Planner

Key Points	Sunday	Monday	Tuesday	Wednesday	Thursday	Friday	Saturday
Remember To Do							

July 20 __ Monthly Planner

Key Points	Sunday	Monday	Tuesday	Wednesday	Thursday	Friday	Saturday
Remember To Do							

August 20__ Monthly Planner

Key Points	Sunday	Monday	Tuesday	Wednesday	Thursday	Friday	Saturday
Remember To Do							

September 20___ Monthly Planner

Key Points	Sunday	Monday	Tuesday	Wednesday	Thursday	Friday	Saturday
Remember To Do							

October 20__ Monthly Planner

Key Points	Sunday	Monday	Tuesday	Wednesday	Thursday	Friday	Saturday
Remember To Do							

November 20__ Monthly Planner

Key Points	Sunday	Monday	Tuesday	Wednesday	Thursday	Friday	Saturday
Key Points							
Remember To Do							

December 20__ Monthly Planner

Key Poinrts	Sunday	Monday	Tuesday	Wednesday	Thursday	Friday	Saturday
Key Poinrts							
Remember To Do							

January 20__ Monthly Planner

Key Points	Sunday	Monday	Tuesday	Wednesday	Thursday	Friday	Saturday
Remember To Do							

January __ - __, 20 __ Weekly Planner

	Sunday	Monday	Tuesday	Wednesday	Thursday	Friday	Saturday
Period Class Time							
Period Class Time							
	Sunday	Monday	Tuesday	Wednesday	Thursday	Friday	Saturday
Period Class Time							

January __ ~ __, 20 __ Weekly Planner

	Sunday	Monday	Tuesday	Wednesday	Thursday	Friday	Saturday
Period Class Time							
	Sunday	Monday	Tuesday	Wednesday	Thursday	Friday	Saturday

January __ - __, 20__ Weekly Planner

	Sunday	Monday	Tuesday	Wednesday	Thursday	Friday	Saturday
Period Class Time							

January __ - __, 20 __ Weekly Planner

	Sunday	Monday	Tuesday	Wednesday	Thursday	Friday	Saturday
Period Class Time							

January __ ~ __, 20__ Weekly Planner

	Sunday	Monday	Tuesday	Wednesday	Thursday	Friday	Saturday
Period Class Time							

February 20__ Monthly Planner

Key Points	Sunday	Monday	Tuesday	Wednesday	Thursday	Friday	Saturday
Remember To Do							

February __ - __, 20__ Weekly Planner

	Sunday	Monday	Tuesday	Wednesday	Thursday	Friday	Saturday
Period Class Time							
Period Class Time							

February __ - __, 20__ Weekly Planner

	Sunday	Monday	Tuesday	Wednesday	Thursday	Friday	Saturday
Period Classs Time							
Period Classs Time	Sunday	Monday	Tuesday	Wednesday	Thursday	Friday	Saturday

February __ - __, 20__ Weekly Planner

	Sunday	Monday	Tuesday	Wednesday	Thursday	Friday	Saturday
Period Class Time							
	Sunday	Monday	Tuesday	Wednesday	Thursday	Friday	Saturday

February __ - __, 20 __ Weekly Planner

	Sunday	Monday	Tuesday	Wednesday	Thursday	Friday	Saturday
Period Class Time							

	Sunday	Monday	Tuesday	Wednesday	Thursday	Friday	Saturday

February __ - __, 20 __ Weekly Planner

	Sunday	Monday	Tuesday	Wednesday	Thursday	Friday	Saturday
Period Class Time							

March 20 _ _ Monthly Planner

Key Points	Sunday	Monday	Tuesday	Wednesday	Thursday	Friday	Saturday
Key Points	Sunday	Monday	Tuesday	Wednesday	Thursday	Friday	Saturday
Remember To Do							

March __ - __, 20__ Weekly Planner

	Sunday	Monday	Tuesday	Wednesday	Thursday	Friday	Saturday
Period Class Time							
Period Class Time							
	Sunday	Monday	Tuesday	Wednesday	Thursday	Friday	Saturday

March __ ~ __, 20 __ Weekly Planner

	Sunday	Monday	Tuesday	Wednesday	Thursday	Friday	Saturday
Period Class Time							
Period Class Time							

March __ – __, 20__ Weekly Planner

	Sunday	Monday	Tuesday	Wednesday	Thursday	Friday	Saturday
Period Class Time							

March __ - __, 20__ Weekly Planner

Period Class Time	Sunday	Monday	Tuesday	Wednesday	Thursday	Friday	Saturday

March __ ~ __, 20__ Weekly Planner

	Sunday	Monday	Tuesday	Wednesday	Thursday	Friday	Saturday
Period Class Time							

	Sunday	Monday	Tuesday	Wednesday	Thursday	Friday	Saturday
Period Class Time							

March __ - __, 20__ Weekly Planner

	Sunday	Monday	Tuesday	Wednesday	Thursday	Friday	Saturday
Period Class Time							

April 20__ Monthly Planner

Key Points	Sunday	Monday	Tuesday	Wednesday	Thursday	Friday	Saturday
Remember To Do							

April __ - __, 20__ Weekly Planner

	Sunday	Monday	Tuesday	Wednesday	Thursday	Friday	Saturday
Period Class Time							

April __ ~ __, 20__ Weekly Planner

	Sunday	Monday	Tuesday	Wednesday	Thursday	Friday	Saturday
Period Class Time							
Period Class Time							

April __ - __, 20__ Weekly Planner

	Sunday	Monday	Tuesday	Wednesday	Thursday	Friday	Saturday
Period Class Time							
	Sunday	Monday	Tuesday	Wednesday	Thursday	Friday	Saturday
Period Class Time							

April __ - __, 20__ Weekly Planner

	Sunday	Monday	Tuesday	Wednesday	Thursday	Friday	Saturday
Period Class Time							
Period Class Time							

April __ - __, 20__ Weekly Planner

	Sunday	Monday	Tuesday	Wednesday	Thursday	Friday	Saturday
Period Class Time							
	Sunday	Monday	Tuesday	Wednesday	Thursday	Friday	Saturday
Period Class Time							

May 20__ Monthly Planner

Key Points	Sunday	Monday	Tuesday	Wednesday	Thursday	Friday	Saturday
Remember To Do							

May __ ~ __, 20__ Weekly Planner

	Sunday	Monday	Tuesday	Wednesday	Thursday	Friday	Saturday
Period Class Time							
	Sunday	Monday	Tuesday	Wednesday	Thursday	Friday	Saturday
Period Class Time							

May __ ~ __, 20__ Weekly Planner

	Sunday	Monday	Tuesday	Wednesday	Thursday	Friday	Saturday
Period Class Time							
	Sunday	Monday	Tuesday	Wednesday	Thursday	Friday	Saturday
Period Class Time							

May __ - __, 20__ Weekly Planner

	Sunday	Monday	Tuesday	Wednesday	Thursday	Friday	Saturday
Period Class Time							
	Sunday	Monday	Tuesday	Wednesday	Thursday	Friday	Saturday
Period Class Time							

May __ ~ __, 20__ Weekly Planner

	Sunday	Monday	Tuesday	Wednesday	Thursday	Friday	Saturday
Period Class Time							
	Sunday	Monday	Tuesday	Wednesday	Thursday	Friday	Saturday
Period Class Time							

May __ - __, 20__ Weekly Planner

	Sunday	Monday	Tuesday	Wednesday	Thursday	Friday	Saturday
Period Class Time							
	Sunday	Monday	Tuesday	Wednesday	Thursday	Friday	Saturday
Period Class Time							

June 20__ Monthly Planner

Key Points	Sunday	Monday	Tuesday	Wednesday	Thursday	Friday	Saturday
	Sunday	Monday	Tuesday	Wednesday	Thursday	Friday	Saturday
Remember To Do							

June __ - __, 20__ Weekly Planner

	Sunday	Monday	Tuesday	Wednesday	Thursday	Friday	Saturday
Period Class Time							
	Sunday	Monday	Tuesday	Wednesday	Thursday	Friday	Saturday
Period Class Time							

June __ - __, 20__ Weekly Planner

	Sunday	Monday	Tuesday	Wednesday	Thursday	Friday	Saturday
Period Class Time							

	Sunday	Monday	Tuesday	Wednesday	Thursday	Friday	Saturday
Period Class Time							

June __ - __, 20__ Weekly Planner

	Sunday	Monday	Tuesday	Wednesday	Thursday	Friday	Saturday
Period Class Time							
	Sunday	Monday	Tuesday	Wednesday	Thursday	Friday	Saturday
Period Class Time							

June __ - __, 20__ Weekly Planner

	Sunday	Monday	Tuesday	Wednesday	Thursday	Friday	Saturday
Period Calls Time							
	Sunday	Monday	Tuesday	Wednesday	Thursday	Friday	Saturday
Period Calls Time							

June __ - __, 20 __ Weekly Planner

	Sunday	Monday	Tuesday	Wednesday	Thursday	Friday	Saturday
Period Class Time							
	Sunday	Monday	Tuesday	Wednesday	Thursday	Friday	Saturday
Period Class Time							

June __ - __, 20__ Weekly Planner

	Sunday	Monday	Tuesday	Wednesday	Thursday	Friday	Saturday
Period Class Time							
	Sunday	Monday	Tuesday	Wednesday	Thursday	Friday	Saturday
Period Class Time							

July 20__ Monthly Planner

Key Points	Sunday	Monday	Tuesday	Wednesday	Thursday	Friday	Saturday
Key Points							
Remember To Do							

July __ - __, 20__ Weekly Planner

	Sunday	Monday	Tuesday	Wednesday	Thursday	Friday	Saturday
Peiod Class Time							
	Sunday	Monday	Tuesday	Wednesday	Thursday	Friday	Saturday
Peiod Class Time							

July __ - __, 20__ Weekly Planner

	Sunday	Monday	Tuesday	Wednesday	Thursday	Friday	Saturday
Peiod Class Time							
	Sunday	Monday	Tuesday	Wednesday	Thursday	Friday	Saturday
Peiod Class Time							

July __ - __, 20__ Weekly Planner

	Sunday	Monday	Tuesday	Wednesday	Thursday	Friday	Saturday
Peiod Class Time							
	Sunday	Monday	Tuesday	Wednesday	Thursday	Friday	Saturday
Peiod Class Time							

July __ ~ __, 20__ Weekly Planner

	Sunday	Monday	Tuesday	Wednesday	Thursday	Friday	Saturday
Peiod Class Time							
	Sunday	Monday	Tuesday	Wednesday	Thursday	Friday	Saturday
Peiod Class Time							

July __ - __, 20__ Weekly Planner

	Sunday	Monday	Tuesday	Wednesday	Thursday	Friday	Saturday
Peiod Class Time							
	Sunday	Monday	Tuesday	Wednesday	Thursday	Friday	Saturday
Peiod Class Time							

August 20__ Monthly Planner

Key Points	Sunday	Monday	Tuesday	Wednesday	Thursday	Friday	Saturday
Remember To Do							

August __ – __, 20__ Weekly Planner

	Sunday	Monday	Tuesday	Wednesday	Thursday	Friday	Saturday
Period Class Time							

	Sunday	Monday	Tuesday	Wednesday	Thursday	Friday	Saturday
Period Class Time							

August __ - __, 20__ Weekly Planner

	Sunday	Monday	Tuesday	Wednesday	Thursday	Friday	Saturday
Period Class Time							

	Sunday	Monday	Tuesday	Wednesday	Thursday	Friday	Saturday
Period Class Time							

August __ - __, 20__ Weekly Planner

	Sunday	Monday	Tuesday	Wednesday	Thursday	Friday	Saturday
Period Class Time							
	Sunday	Monday	Tuesday	Wednesday	Thursday	Friday	Saturday
Period Class Time							

August __ – __, 20__ Weekly Planner

	Sunday	Monday	Tuesday	Wednesday	Thursday	Friday	Saturday
Period Class Time							
	Sunday	Monday	Tuesday	Wednesday	Thursday	Friday	Saturday
Period Class Time							

August __ - __, 20 __ Weekly Planner

	Sunday	Monday	Tuesday	Wednesday	Thursday	Friday	Saturday
Period Class Time							
	Sunday	Monday	Tuesday	Wednesday	Thursday	Friday	Saturday
Period Class Time							